Professional
Kitchen Design

THE UNTOLD REALITY

*THE UNTOLD REALITIES OF HOW TO
CREATE AND MAINTAIN A
PROFITABLE, PROFESSIONAL KITCHEN*
VOLUME III

Professional
Kitchen Design

THE UNTOLD REALITY

Tristan B. Jones

Special thanks to Christopher Morris at Vice Design for the awesome cover art. You can reach him at

www.vicedesign.co

Contents

There is some room in the back for you to start sketching your own designs/notes.

Intro

Designing your kitchen is the single most important aspect of opening a new restaurant. Every little detail is important, from what equipment you purchase to where you place it, to kitchen noise levels and what your employees stand on, will ultimately either hinder or help you in service. These decisions could lead to a happy staff and a profitable kitchen or a disaster every service.

You also have to realize you can't design a kitchen until you have your concept nailed down. This is a mistake I see owners make regularly. They hire a chef without having their own expectations laid out for themselves, much less the prospective hire. You can't just buy an oven and a range and hope everything will be ok. The kind of food you will be serving will determine what equipment you will ultimately need.

I am aware this might seem obvious, but after noticing there are almost no resources out there for people trying to design their new restaurant kitchen, I thought I could help.

Tristan B. Jones

When Does the Process Start

First off, make sure you have the money. I can't tell you how many people I have seen fail to open their dream establishment because they ran out of funds in the process. It is hard to say how much you need to get a place going, as there are so many factors to look at. So I can't give you a bulk standard answer. This will depend on the type of food you want to serve, whether or not you are building a kitchen from scratch or taking over the lease at a place with most of the equipment you need, as well as a laundry list of other issues.

I have seen some disasters when starting new restaurants. I once worked for a company that spent $120,000 dollars on two hand-carved bars shipped in from Alaska before the front or back of the house were little more than concrete. They never opened. They ran out of money before the first piece of equipment was installed. Don't be these people.

You need to realize what is most important to get your business going. The more time you take and money you spend before you open your doors, the longer it will take you to get back in the black. With an average restaurant taking over a year after opening to reach this point, there is no time or money to waste.

The first thing you need to do is get a chef. Many owners will try to find a location, start building a kitchen, and then put out an ad for a chef. This is a rookie mistake. You can end up spending tens or hundreds of thousands of dollars on useless equipment. You need find a chef that understands what you are trying to accomplish before you do anything else. Does this apply to a place that only sells snow cones? No, obviously not, but even if you are just selling hamburgers, you will need a chef. Once you have your kitchen/menu properly designed and costed out, you can hire a line cook and make him kitchen manager. By that point, you will have spent enough time with your chef to learn how everything works.

The other books in this series can also help with this.

PROFESSIONAL KITCHEN DESIGN

Once you have a chef, and both of you fully understand the concept you as the owner are shooting for, you can build some mock menus you are both happy with. This is the easiest way to start looking at what equipment you will need. Will you have a lot of sautéed items? Will you be baking all of your desserts? Will a lot of your meat be sous vide? These are the kinds of questions that will ultimately determine what equipment is needed.

This will also give you an idea of what size space you will need. You need to know what stations will be working where, and why. You can buy all the necessary equipment for a menu, but if your kitchen is so small you can only fit two staff members in it at a time, and you have one hundred seats in your restaurant, good luck serving anything of substantial quality in a reasonable amount of time.

This is why you need a professional. Every decision you make from day one will ultimately determine your success, and if you try to save money by starting the process yourself, odds are you will waste a lot of time and money in the process. Even after reading a book like this, the gaps in your knowledge will be far too large to simply ignore. I will go over what I can, but nothing can get you the knowledge you need without the experience.

Your Professional Help

The chef you hire is very important. You will be spending copious amounts of time with him/her, so make sure you choose wisely. There are also other routes you can take, but I suggest a well-trained competent chef.

You could, for example, hire restaurant consultants. Now I can't speak ill of the profession, as I have held this title many times, but I have seen my fair share of con artists. These are people who tell you they know everything necessary, they even have a neat little CV, but in the end, they will just take your money and run leaving you with a substandard establishment.

I witnessed this first hand in Texas. Two people were hired to open a place, and it became painfully clear they didn't have a clue. Unfortunately, the owner was new to the game himself, so he had no idea he was being swindled. It is very easy for someone to preach being a professional, so be careful. They took that owner for over $150,000 before the restaurant finally opened and they disappeared. The place lasted about six months after they left, but the damage had been done. The time it was in operation was just the owner throwing money at the problem.

Are restaurant consultants a viable option? Of course, but I wouldn't recommend it. I say this as a consultant has set up many successful establishments, just hear me out. If you are looking for someone with plenty of knowledge about opening restaurants, why would you hire and work with someone who will leave after opening? They have no real stake in the game. This doesn't mean they would intentionally try to harm your business, but if they have no stake in the game, why would they care. This is a very nihilistic view, but it is something to consider.

With a chef however, you can bring them in at the beginning, pay them well, as no one helping you open a restaurant will be cheap, and they will stick with you till the end. This is usually the capacity I work at. I come in to help open the business, and later become the chef. There is no disconnect in this scenario. Your restaurant consultant might have ten years of GM experience, but never being a chef, they don't know what is actually necessary to produce sous vide rabbit with sweet potato hash and rabbit jus.

This is horrible for any chef you try to bring in after the fact. You want to have seven different kinds of whole roasted fish on the menu and you have one broiler set up and no convection oven. I've seen it ladies and gentleman. Do yourself a favor, get a chef, and work together from day one. I cannot stress this enough.

Who Do You Trust

So why are there almost no resources out there to help? The short answer is simply when someone is spending the kind of money it takes to build a professional kitchen; there will always be people around to 'help'.

Who are these people? Well we have gone over restaurant consultants and chefs, but let's look at the scum of the earth. Now it can't be all of them, but let me give you a scenario.

You want to open your restaurant, so you find a location and secure it. Good for you. You obviously didn't read the first two chapters, but stay with me. Now you need equipment. Almost all people opening a restaurant do the same thing. They contact their local used restaurant equipment 'specialist'. These people. Now look, I know, not every used car salesman is a crook, just like not all of these people are crooks. But in my experience, if you walk in there blind as an owner that has never been through this process, you will get ripped to shreds. I know what you're thinking, 'I will be pragmatic, make conscientious decisions, and be careful, I'll be fine'. NO, YOU WONT. Trust me on this. I've seen it too many times.

I've bumped heads with so many of these guys it's hard to count, and they are ruthless. You tell them what you are looking for; give them dimensions for the space, and hold on to your hat because the crap that they bring back might as well be smeared on toilet paper.

Watch them as they explain what everything is. You want a combi oven? We have this one with three racks. You want a bigger one? Oh, sorry, they only come in this size unless you go straight convection. Just because they don't have what you are looking for, you must get this item. Don't fall for it, owners do all the time. 'Well Tristan, he said we have to get that'. Forget that guy, no you don't. You take that and add on the fact that there will be 5 pieces of equipment that you don't even want. 'Oh that's the sheeter'. 'Why is there a sheeter Ted?', you'll ask. They always have the same three ways to dance around it, either, 'Oh, I thought you wanted one', or, 'Oh how did that get on there?', or, 'Well you'll need it because...' The whole time the owner is lapping up the bile of a sycophantic sociopath. They are crooks, this is obviously more of a used equipment problem, but it happens with both new and used. Watch them closely.

Sorry about my rant. The point is, you need someone who is knowledgeable about all aspects of the kitchen. That might be a good price on a combi oven, but if you will have to rip up the foundation to put in a drain for it, you might just blow too much of your budget because that's what Ted had in stock. Take this problem and add a very expensive consultant that has never actually cooked anything, and you might as well start lighting hundred dollar bills on fire.

I'm not saying a used equipment guy isn't a good option, they are. They are where I always start when beginning to design a kitchen. They can provide very useful services that could be drastically more expensive otherwise such as drawing up the blueprints you need for your contractor. I'm simply stating that if you are new, do not try to go it alone, or you will end up hurting your own bank account in the long run.

So who do you trust? Your chef, plain and simple. If you have a restaurant consultant that used to be a chef, that's ok, at least he will get everything right so when you hire your permanent chef, he doesn't wonder why the kitchen design was drawn in crayon. It would be a shame to spend all that time and money only to have your new chef quit after two months because of the atrocious state of the design.

Stations

Now you have a mock menu or two, and you need to decide on what equipment is necessary. This is a much simpler task when broken down into stations. Let's use a basic set up as an example.

The brigade system is the backbone of all kitchens. Auguste Escoffier is the man who invented the system around the turn of the twentieth century. This is what is in place in almost every kitchen in the world. The concept came from his time in the French military during World War I. It was devised as a way to delegate tasks in an orderly fashion as a way to comprehensively control an entire operation in a descending pyramid. At the top, you have the Executive Chef, the man, the boss, the big cheese. He knows every nut and bolt of his operation and can tell you exactly what is happening in his kitchen at any time. Under him, you have the Executive Sous Chef, sous, in French, means under. He is literally under the exec on the pyramid.

PROFESSIONAL KITCHEN DESIGN

When the exec would like to make a policy change or add a dish, he deals directly with his exec sous, who then passes the information down the ladder until it gets to the necessary department. Under exec sous, you have the Head Chef, or Chef de Cuisine. From there, there are many other departments, the Chef de Charcuterie, in charge of meats, the Chef de Garde Manger, in charge of the cold section, pastry, and many others under them depending on the size of your establishment. Of course, not every operation is large enough to have all these positions, so in a normal restaurant, you have a Head Chef and a Sous at the top, followed by your cooks in respective stations.

There might be an Exec off property somewhere, but an exec chef's job title is there because he is in charge of more than one operation. For example, if your operation a single restaurant but is large enough for an exec, not only will you be doing normal services, but you will also have a catering department, and the exec is in charge of both. If you only have one restaurant serving dinner, you only need a head, if you have three restaurants you have an exec, and three heads. I will be discussing the basics of a normal sized kitchen in a normal sized restaurant to simplify. For example, we will not be discussing a chef de charcuterie with cooks under him, we will keep it elementary.

You do need to understand this system before trying to set up your kitchen. Trying to figure out who is responsible for what duty at any given time on any given day will frustrate you and your staff.

Here is a mock menu along with daily specials such as whole fish and fresh seafood for an Italian restaurant, something upscale but not too crazy. Then we will look at the stations, considering what they will need and why.

PROFESSIONAL KITCHEN DESIGN

Salads
Mixed salad
Burrata and arugula
Caponatta and Foccacia

Starters
Pork Belly with Cauliflower
Tuna Tartar
Zucchini Flowers with Brandada
Vitello Tonnato

Mains
Paccheri, Calamari
Octopus with Carrot
Rabbit, Cabbage and Gnocci
Lamb Saddle, Brussel Sprouts
Herbed Veal, Smoked Potato Puree

Sides
Zucchini Fritte
Roasted Veg
Pecorino Polenta

Specials
Roasted Snapper for Two
Monk Fish Meuniere for Two
Prime Black Angus I-Bone
Pork Cheeks, Asparagus
Lobster Spaghetti for Two
Truffle Risotto

Desserts
Strawberry Soufflé
Chocolate Fondant
Assorted Bites

This is a small, workable menu, and you and your chef have agreed this is the *style* of food you would like to do. Remember, nothing is permanent, but you have to have your concept ready before you move forward. So, if you agree with each other, let's look at the stations.

Garde Manger

The cold station. Your cold station generally needs the most individual small chilled items. Usually, they will have what some call a 'sandwich prep' table. I will mention now, although kitchen equipment does have names for everything, they can vary, so let's not get too hung up on what to call what.

Your sandwich prep table is essentially a box that comes up to average kitchen table height, around thirty-six inches. There is a small work surface in front, with a lid that can be lifted behind it. in that lid you can fit your hotel pans, usually sixth or ninth but some can fit full, and they will stay cold. Below, there will be doors to hold back up prep. How big of one do you need? Well let's look at the menu.

All of the salads will be coming from here, so how many items does that entail? Well, you have your insalata mista, your mixed salad, let's say that is comprised of a basic mesclun mix. Mixed with that you have roasted red peppers, halved cherry tomatoes, toasted almonds, and crumbled feta. Most will keep the salad below, but if you put it up top, you just lost a lot of space, if you sell a lot however, it might be necessary. So let's say you have a half pan of greens, plus four more ingredients, and vinaigrette. That is half pan for salad, sixth pan for sauces, and four ninth pan for extras. Considering usually these come in sizes that will fit a full pan per, you are already out of space on the small model. That's just one dish.

Maybe you are keeping the salad below, that's fine by me, but there's more. You have burrata, arugula, vitello tonnato and accompaniments, capponatta, and are you doing an amuse bouche? All of these dishes all have garnishes and extras that go along with them.

This is how the cold station racks up so much storage space when compared to other stations. For this menu I would recommend a minimum of sixty inches, and that is still pushing it. I would go larger if you could.

Grill

I say grill, but in this scenario, there will not be a grill. It's just another blanket industry term. We will say chef de charcuterie. The meat guy.

You will obviously need either a fridge or some low-boys for this station, but probably both. There are sauces, purees, jus', demi glace, sides such as roasted veg, and more to be taken into account. In essence, this station will need everything from an oven to a range, but you can pass on the fryer. We'll leave that to the guy on sauté.

For speed and ease of service, I recommend a flat top. You can brown veggies and octopus on it quickly, as well as steaks. Could you use a pan for these? Of course you can, but you are adding onto your dish machine budget immensely by doing so and slowing down service.

You will also need an oven. There are a lot of options out there, and I can't tell you one is leaps and bounds above all the rest, but if I had to pick one, any chef would agree, Rational is a solid bet. Don't go cheap on your oven. If you get a good one in the first place, you will save a lot of headache later. A good combi (combination steam and heat) oven is your best friend. You can take meat, the rabbit for example, vac pack it and sous vide it in your oven over night, or when you get there in the morning. Just pop it on half steam half heat and go to town. This makes the quality of your product go up while ticket times and labor costs stay down. I would also suggest a speed rack under the oven, for ease of service.

He will of course need burners, for heating up the different sauces and purees. Personally, I like a good French top for this, but they can be expensive. These are the kinds of things you need to discuss with your chef. I can't stand it when I'm told money is no issue, and yet when I pick out equipment, it becomes an issue. As an owner, you need to be up front about your budget.

You have to remember, because the grill guy will be preparing a lot of main courses, he will need a lot of refrigerator space. The cold station may have more individual items, but the meat guy needs more real estate. All of those whole fish and t-bones have to go somewhere, and if you think he/she will be running to the walk in every time, you are sorely mistaken.

Sauté

Your sauté guy is going to be running the pasta's, fried foods, risottos, etc. They will need room for plenty of pans going at once. Again, I prefer the french top, but it can be done with burners. He will need a minimum of eight burners just for his station. Don't be one of those owners that has eight for the whole kitchen and everyone has to share. Sharing is caring but not on the line. You don't have time to deal with asking someone if it ok to move their sauce so you can heat up yours.

They will also need the fryer. Almost every kitchen in the world has a way to fry things. How big it is and what station it is on will depend on your menu. Obviously, there are not many fried items on this menu, so you won't need an excessive piece of equipment, but never, ever buy the smallest cheapest fryer. There are a few reasons, let me explain.

Personally, I only go gas. They heat up faster and hold temps better during service. They are also cheaper to buy and run. If at all possible, go gas. The size is extremely important as well. If you are running a burger joint using frozen fries, you better have a monster of a fryer. Every time you drop something cold, the fryer temperature has to bounce back or you end up with soggy greasy food. The larger the size, the less it will need to bounce back. I'm not saying you need a monster for this menu, but buying the smallest fifteen pound countertop model is a waste of money. Don't go smaller than thirty pounds in my book, but maybe that's just me.

He will of course need low boys and a fridge as well. How this will configure into your kitchen depends on your space and what is available. Every kitchen is a snowflake my friends, there is never one simple answer. He will have to have his precooked risotto rice, sauces, and lobsters.

He won't need as much space as grill, but he will need a good amount.

Pastry

Your pastry chef generally lives in a world of their own. As such they will need their own equipment. I know if you are an owner looking at your budget right now you are not happy to hear this, but it's true. No one wants their strawberry soufflé baking next to a whole snapper, or lamb. On top of that, who's to say the pastry guy needs the same temperature as your grill guy?

Luckily, you can generally get away with a smaller oven for pastry. I don't recommend this, though. If you are buying a second oven, it's better to bite the bullet and get another decent sized one. It doesn't need to be floor to ceiling, just average four or five racks. I can guarantee you, if you are running a restaurant like this successfully, at some point your grill guy will need to borrow the pastry oven either for service or prep.

Pastry will need one or two burners as well, but you don't need to go crazy and buy another range. He will not be cooking most items to order, and even if he does, it will be in an oven. Usually I just buy a couple of induction burners. This keeps the heat down as he may not have a hood anywhere other than over the oven, but also allows for maximum control for things like candy making.

Dealing with ice creams and sorbets he will need some low boys that freeze, as well as refrigerated for garnish. Depending on how extensive your pastry menu is, and how good your chef is, you might need more space than your cold station. But it depends on you and what you would like your pastry section to produce.

The Pass

When I say the pass, I'm talking about the guy on expo. He calls the tickets out, and makes sure that everything leaves the kitchen without mistakes. Generally, this is handled by the chef. On the pass you will of course need hot plates, as well as different garnishes and sauces. The easiest way to keep all of this in order is a steam well. If you are serving green peppercorn demi-glace with every I-bone, and you sell thirty a night, you can just keep that sauce warm on the pass. Countertop models are preferable here, as they can be moved freeing up the most valuable countertop space when needed.

Garnishing on the pass needs to be flexible. Some menus might have seven heated sauces with crunchy toppings, some might have two frozen and and five powdered. The pass can change drastically with each menu, even though you have a concept, don't limit your pass by installing permanent equipment when a cheaper easier countertop might suffice.

At this point I will mention, in this set up, most plating will be done by the chef. The rest of the staff is capable, but why would you not want your chef to plate? It is, of course, always a team effort, but when you get busy, it's nice to let the cooks focus on cooking. They can just drop off the food that is ready to go, and the chef can plate it.

Our Little Example

I want you to remember, that was one example of one kitchen. This is not the end all be all of how to run a kitchen. I have based this one example off of one kitchen I felt had a good set up.

The importance of this mental experiment was simply to show how crucial it is to know how your kitchen will run *before* you start buying equipment and designing. Trying to rush into things without the proper knowledge will have you end up with a kitchen that is not only inefficient, but dangerous.

Speaking of dangerous, let's look at flow.

Flow

How your kitchen flows will determine how fast or slow your ticket times are, as well as how many people you need and what you are capable of producing.

To begin deciding how your kitchen will operate, first you have to bring up the recurring theme in this book. Nail down your concept. If you are thinking about opening a restaurant, I suggest going out to eat as often as possible and seeing how other people are accomplishing goals similar to yours.

This is like an education that comes with food. If you want to open a burger joint, go eat at a lot of burger joints. If you want to go more upscale, go to upscale joints. Try to find places with open kitchens, so you can observe.

Odds are, if you spend enough time observing, you will begin to notice some good and some bad systems, so what should you look for?

The Bad

Well to start, we'll look at some of the bad. Every station should have a hand sink available somewhere close by. Not every station needs their own, but if you start observing at restaurants you will begin to notice, all that stuff about hand washing can get lost pretty fast in a rush. I see it all the time in kitchens and it still bothers me after all these years. One of the main reasons people don't wash their hands is the fact that the hand sink is on the other side of the kitchen and they're busy. I don't agree with it, but I will attest that poor kitchen design plays a roll.

You will also begin to notice the runners. I don't mean food runners, I mean the restaurants that you can see in the kitchen and there seems to always be one or two people running to the back. This is another flaw in kitchen design. Sometimes, it might be because they got hit hard and didn't have enough prep, but not always. Sometimes it's simple because of lack of fridge space. This interrupts the flow of the kitchen leading to increased ticket times and unhappy cooks.

Did you notice the lack of heat lamps on the pass? Heat lamps can kill food, yes, very quickly, but that becomes a server issue if it becomes a repetitive problem. People go to a restaurant to enjoy their meal, if it's not hot, why bother. They are only a necessary evil because it is not possible to have a server standing at the pass every time a plate hits it. So you need something to keep it warm.

How many ticket machines do they have? This one can be a point of contention. Generally, the higher up in price point at a restaurant or the more 'fine dining' it is, the less ticket machines you have. Generally, the chef will call out all orders followed by a "Heard" from the people he was speaking to. This is a time honored tradition. This is because the higher up you go; the more people in that kitchen want to be a chef. The lower you go, no one cares, they are there for a paycheck, so remembering everything called to them is not a point of pride, it's more of a nuisance.

PROFESSIONAL KITCHEN DESIGN

Nether system is right or wrong, but having people staring at their own ticket doing their own work makes it hard to properly communicate. When a table of four orders food, they don't want one person's ready ten minutes before everyone else's because that cook is only focusing on his/her work. Sadly, this happens all too often.

People constantly bumping into each other is a horrifying prospect. With all the dangers in a kitchen, from hot oil and pans to knives, people getting in each other's way can be extremely dangerous. This is the backbone of a poorly designed kitchen. Unsafe is a mild way to put it, but you would be surprised how often you will see kitchens with no flow.

The Good

Surely it's not all doom and gloom right? Odds are, some of the restaurants you will go to will be well run establishments. The purpose of this exercise is to train yourself to see the difference. So what are some good things you can notice?

First off, rhythm. A proper kitchen will have a rhythm, like a ballet. Everyone will seem to be in unison, completing different tasks, yet all ending with the same result. There should not be a frantic seizure like vibe to how the kitchen moves. When your party of four's plates come to the pass, there should be multiple stations coming to the pass at the same time. All of them should be bringing their different dishes from their respective stations all landing at once.

As mentioned before, they should not be running around the kitchen like a chicken with its head cut off. They should be, generally, staying on their station, working it smoothly, without interruption.

You should see communication between the different stations. If you see a kitchen with five different stations and no one is talking to each other, they have lost their flow. You are back to a kitchen where 'you put your food up and I'll put mine up when it's ready' is the attitude. This should all be timed and communicated.

What it all means

What all of this boils down to is a choke point. You have your leader, your chef, or whoever your expo person is calling tickets and getting everything out. They need to be able to communicate to every corner of the kitchen.

All the madness and effort you spent the last chunk of your life to create goes from the station to the pass, gets plated, and the last drop of sauce is put on. Your chef is responsible for that finished product. All of the planning comes down to who stands in that choke point position and how much time and effort was put into helping them and the team, succeed.

The Conclusion

The flow of the kitchen needs to be well planned out. You are probably working with a competent chef at this point, so use a mock menu, and run through a day of prep, service, and cleandown with that menu. You don't need to get too detailed, but I bet you find some problems. If you thought you

could just buy equipment and be done with
it, you can, but I don't suggest it.

Floors

Beyond equipment, you need to consider what your staff will be standing on. Kitchen floors are constantly covered in grease and slippery pieces of food that fell when no one was looking. These can lead to horrendous accidents and put you at risk as the proprietor.

All staff should be wearing non slip shoes regardless of position, but with the right floors, you can make sure you have done everything in your power to prevent accidents. Here are your options for flooring in your new kitchen.

Ceramic Tiles

Most kitchens go with ceramic tiles. This is a decent option, and is the choice for many around the world. As with all options on this front, they are heat resistant, and hold up well. You can even get some slightly textured options to help with the non-slip capabilities of the product. Personally, I'm not a fan of grout. You will be deck brushing your floors regularly regardless, but most cooks have memories of scrubbing the same area of grout trying to get a french fry that has been mercilessly pressed into a crack.

That being said, it is number one for a reason. It is easily fit into any space and lasts for a very long time. On the down side, on dropped pot can crack a tile, leading to build up. It's a real shame when someone gets a negative mark on a health inspection because of this, especially if the owner just spent a lot of money on a new floor.

Brick

Brick is a great option for an open kitchen, if you want to look snazzy. It holds up well, but it needs to be glazed with a protective coating, adding to your cost. I have personally never built a kitchen with brick, but hey, it looks nice right?

I would say you can look into this option if you have an open kitchen, where your clients will all see it and you want it to be pretty. For most kitchens, however, even with an opening to allow customers to see in, the floor is usually not in view. So your call.

Stone

Stone looks amazing. We can start with that. There are different options on what stones you can use, so you can really get a look you want. You can even opt for a special brush pattern to enhance the aesthetics, but this is not really a viable option for most.

The problem is the hefty price tag. This is the most expensive option I know of. I honestly can't think of a single reason to go with stone, unless you have too much money to care, in which case that's awesome for you, I'd like to see some pictures of the finished product.

Vinyl

Last but certainly not least, vinyl. Vinyl floors are by far my favorite, next to tile. Both are cheap and easy to install, relatively speaking, but vinyl has the added beneficial option of having no seams.

Seams would be the one issue I have with vinyl. If not installed properly, they do have a tendency to pull up at the seams. Most of the time, the company installing the material will have the capability to do the whole space in one sheet, making this a non-issue. Sometimes you have to ask, so make sure you do.

This also makes it very easy to create a seamless slope running up the wall. One of the hardest parts of keeping a restaurant kitchen floor clean is where it hits the wall. With vinyl, this is not a problem. You can have whoever is installing it run the slope up the wall, and never have to worry about it. This is one of my favorite parts.

Because vinyl contours to the floor, as long as your foundation done properly it is relatively quick and easy to install. You can even get padding to go underneath to help your chef's feet.

Anyone who has felt this for the first time knows how amazing it can be after spending your whole life on tile. Besides, next time your staff complains about pain due to long hours, you can let them know you did everything you could.

PROFESSIONAL KITCHEN DESIGN

Curb Mounts

Curb mounts are another great way to do your floors. Basically, a curb mount is where you set your equipment behind your floor. So you will have the same benefit you had by running your flooring up the wall, all over your kitchen. With vinyl, this creates what is essentially a bucket, where everything flows to your drain. It truly is a beautiful thing.

You do need to make sure the equipment you are buying allow for curb mounting. You don't want to have all of your installers show up only to find out your low boy isn't made to operate under those conditions. You have to make sure you communicate with both the flooring company as well as the equipment company if you would like this to go smoothly.

Mats

Floor mats. Some of you reading this will know what I'm talking about and others will not, so I'll explain them quickly. There are multiple kinds out there, some relatively thin, and not really useful for anything. The most common, that for some reason have made their way into every country I've cooked in, are about an inch thick, black, and have a honeycomb hexagonal pattern.

The benefits are supposedly the same as the cushioned vinyl, but it doesn't take too much imagination to envision what they look like after a shift. Yes they are slightly squishy but I'd rather stand on needles all day. When you take them out to hose off at night you are left carrying a heavy disgusting product that in no way should ever be allowed in a kitchen.

This is a personal opinion, and I'm sure you will find someone out there that disagrees and loves the mats. I can guarantee you; they are not the ones cleaning them. Don't use mats, don't be a monster.

Floors, Conclusion

Personally, I don't think you can go wrong with either vinyl or tile. I always go vinyl when designing a kitchen simply because of the price point, but I have done openings where we know we would be buying new pieces of equipment later, so we went ceramic.

The choice is completely up to you, just make sure you have enough drains that work properly, or you will have cooks walking out with trench foot.

Walls

Good Kitchen walls need to serve two purposes. They need to last, and they need to be able to be cleaned easily. Your choice of what material to use strictly based on what you can afford or should allow in the budget.

Let's look at your options.

Stainless Steel

By far the nicest walls you can get for your kitchen, stainless steel is the most expensive option. You will almost always see stainless steel walls with heat protection behind equipment like flat tops and French tops, but to use this everywhere would be astronomically expensive. This is why you almost never see a professional kitchen that is shiny all the way around the room. You can also get different brush designs and really get a nice custom look.

You need to make sure you have a lengthy conversation with your contractor as to how the stainless will be affixed. I have seen some horrors behind stainless steel plates. The problem is most contractors will agree to do the stainless but want to be as cost effective as possible to lower your cost and maximize their profits. A bad install might just be plates of stainless drilled into studs. You create a micro biome of insects and rodents living off of your product. So again, be careful.

I don't suggest this option because of the price. The outcome is amazing; you have a whole kitchen of an almost indestructible material. Easy to clean and maintain, it really is ideal. The problem with putting that much money into the installation would put your business in the red for much longer than what is advisable. Some would argue that you are investing in a property that you bought and you are upping the resale value of said investment. Sadly, you aren't. The only way you will see a penny of that investment back is if you have an open kitchen. A nice shiny open kitchen will get people to open their wallets, but if it's in the back no one will care.

I find it very difficult to come up with justifications for this kind of expenditure, but this leads us to our next, second most expensive option...

Tile

Tile is a solid choice. It seals the wall tightly as to prevent infestations and leaks. It is fairly durable, and fairly easy to clean. I say fairly because as far as viable walls are concerned, tile is a decent choice, but it has two huge downfalls.

As stated previously, it is *fairly* durable. It is prone to cracking and chipping. Find me a kitchen with tile walls and I'll show you some cracked wall tiles. I don't just mean a hairline crack, I mean a full on hole that looks like someone hit it with a hammer. When you are constantly moving heavy hot equipment around, this will happen. You are delusional if you install this and tell everyone to 'be careful'. As an owner, if you install a kitchen with a tile wall, then proceed to get angry when you see someone damaged a tile, you are truly deranged. They will get broken, deal with it.

Second, is the cleaning. Again, I would use the word *fairly*. The problem lies not with the tile itself, but the grout. If you lightly clean the walls on a weekly schedule maybe with some degreaser and towels it will last a long time. That's great for a cold prep station. The problem is when you have food being cooked near it. A layer of grease will slowly form discoloring your wall and become near impossible to clean. You can easily get the offending substance off of the tile, but the grout is another monster. You have to scrub it vigorously with a stiff brush. This slowly eats away at the grout, until you break through it. You could of course clean it with a clean rag and vinegar every day, and this will hold the problem off for a long time. Eventually, however, it will need to be replaced.

So how long will it last? That depends on the restaurant. If you have a three hundred seat steak house that is busy five days a week filling all those seats then I give tile three years in certain areas. The speed necessary to work the line in this kind of operation means someone will inevitably put a pot of soup or some other delicious concoction on a counter too fast and hit a tile. It is inevitable. So if you make your kitchen all tile, you will have some broken fairly soon after install. I'd take a bet on that any day.

That said fixing tile is no small issue. It involves cutting out old tile and installing new ones. This is a dusty disaster that your kitchen has to be closed for. Most restaurants don't take days off, and can't afford to. 'They can do it at night' you're thinking. Well good luck hiring a contractor at night, if you find one, he will charge you through the nose.

The install itself is no small feat. It takes lots of time and lots of highly skilled man hours to do the job properly. Your contractor might charge you fourty-eight dollars and hour for the install, but he is getting charged thirty-seven by his sub-contractor. Make no mistake my friend, tile work is extremely difficult to do properly.

These sad facts of life do inherently bring along the reality of affecting your resale value. I am not the only one who cringes when I'm looking at a perspective venue and see a wall of white shiny squares waiting to be crushed. I immediately consider the cost of replacing at least the important parts of the wall when budgeting a location.

So when should you use tile? If you can get a good deal and don't put it in the hot areas or dish. This is the equivalent of putting a band-aid on a hatchet wound. If you go tile because of money, odds are you can't afford to open a restaurant regardless.

FRP

FRP or Fire Resistant Paneling is a great option. It comes in many different colors and textures, but the cheapest and easiest is white. Usually, it has a texture, like an alligator skin, but can be smooth. It is cheap, easy to install, and easy to clean. It is just flat paneling that can be fitted to any wall. Because it comes in sheets, it can be custom cut and fit around all pipes and connections. It also goes great with curb mounting. Just make sure you speak with your contractor about limiting the space between the paneling and the wall, as these gaps can be a haven for roaches. Not all glues will work as a solution either, as some glues can be food for the little buggers.

With a great price point, it is always the first option I look at when deciding on walls. In most countries, you can get it installed quite easily. Having worked in countries that this was not an option, sometimes you end up with...

Other

There are obviously more than three options when it comes to your kitchen walls. Heck you can cover your walls with tinfoil for all I care, but those are the big three. Other options include things like cement and concrete that are ridiculously hard to clean. How about brick? Again, same thing. Pyrex/Glass? This can be a great option. I worked in a place once that had a Pyrex wall behind a wood burning grill. It was great, but to do a whole kitchen, no. Too expensive, and what would be behind the glass anyway. Painted? You can't clean paint. Adobe? Look I'll stop here, you get the point. There are more than three options, these are just the first three I seriously consider when setting up a kitchen.

So what do I think?

Well, for me the best answer is a combination. Stainless around the hot areas, stoves, flat tops ect, and FRP around the rest of the kitchen. You can put tile in places that look nice and even cheaper vinyl fake tile sheets in some storage places. It's all about keeping material and labor costs down while getting a kitchen that will last. So talk to your contractor, see what he can do with his crew and what will need to be sub-contracted. Find out about the costs for all, and find a solution that works for you.

Doors

Doors are one of those little details that sometimes go under the radar. I have seen multimillion dollar projects that were amazing down to the tiniest details, but the doors were ridiculous. I did a project kind of like this in Europe once. There was more wrong with this than the door, and maybe we can get into that later. This might give you an idea of why door placement is important.

First, let me show you the plans.

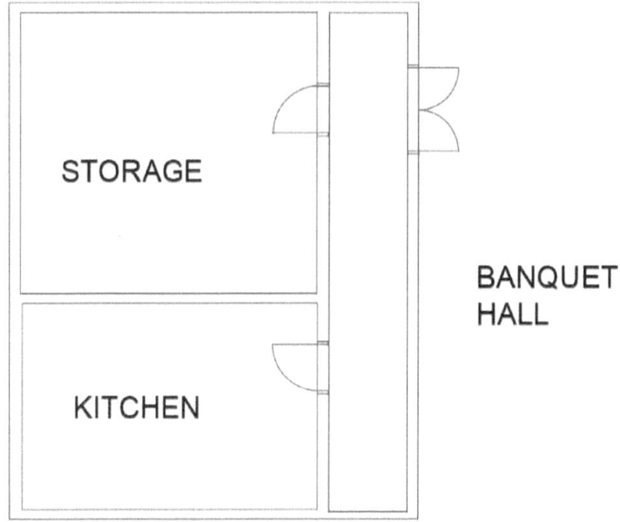

Do you know what is wrong with the door to the kitchen?

Well to start there is only one. That many people need a lot of food. With all of the food coming from one door, you have an engineered nightmare. You would lose hundreds of dollars of food a year just from dropped items, which were dropped simply because of people coming and going. Consider how much food two hundred and fifty people can eat, then put all of it in a door frame. I'm just trying to convey the logistical nightmare that comes with limited access to the kitchen. Banquets and events have start times when everyone shows up. It simply takes too long to get everything out. You can make menus to combat the problem, such as having a lot of items that can sit at room temp for extended periods, but I'm not going into a deep dive on how I would work with this horrendous set up. I'm glad I was brought in when I was, or I would have been stuck with that train wreck of a design.

The doors to the banquet hall were another issue. Both doors only open and close in one direction. On top of that when I say close, I mean you need to use a mechanism to open them. You would have waiters with full hands constantly trying to open doors. If you think that's ok, try to do it yourself. Then do it for ten hours a day every day.

I realize that some people are saying, 'most kitchens have one door', and for small to medium size normal services you could have one, but I don't suggest it. You will have people dropping things and getting hurt trying to go in as people come out and vice versa. Your front of house needs to be able to flow as well. This means a door for in and a door for out with clear walkways to the pass for both. There has to be a system that is convenient for front of the house to come into the kitchen, get food, then leave without worrying about bumping into people.

Make sure you are taking door placement and direction as seriously as you would any other part of design. I know if I have to spend another hour trying to explain to another rich owner why there design has to be scrapped because of a door I might lose it.

Open Kitchens

Now you want an open kitchen too!? Ok, so you have a great design idea for an open kitchen. Be honest, you saw something like it somewhere and now you want to copy it. I've seen it before. Regardless, the question is how do you maintain flow while keeping the part of the kitchen you want people to see visible?

It depends on what experience you want for your customer. Do you want just the pass open so people can see your lovely plating? How about a nice view of your wood fired grill, or pizza oven? Maybe you want to have the hot line right in front of people as they eat. How about a fully open concept with the whole line in front of the whole restaurant?

All are possible, each one just has a slightly different solution. There is never a one size fits all solution for any kitchen design issue. This is mostly due to the fact that all spaces are different. So let's look at how you can accomplish the same end results with the concepts factored in.

On the pass

This is probably the easiest to pull off. All you need is a wall with a hole cut in it. Cut it where it is about four feet tall and go to the ceiling, or not all the way to the ceiling, up to you. You can make it any shape as long as you can get plates through it. Place a stainless steel shelf and that's about all you need. That is now your pass, congratulations. You can also put glass or Pyrex, just leave a gap about a foot and a half tall. The glass can also help protect noise from the kitchen, but we will discuss that later. Also, you can get markers to write things on the glass like specials, or maybe a smiley face.

Now that I'm writing this I think that might be the only easy to explain issue in the entire three book collection.

Showing off Equipment

So many owners want to spend big on a fancy piece of equipment and show it off to all that come into the establishment. I have seen this done well, but I've also seen it blow so much of the budget on such ridiculous expenditures they never even get to open.

I get it, you paid to fly some guy in from Italy to make you an oven and you want to show it off. I can appreciate that. When done correctly its beautiful to be able to show off something cool like that.

How do you pull it off tastefully? It depends on the equipment, so I can give some examples. I mentioned earlier the grill with the glass back. This is a great way to show fire. Because the rule is, if you can show fire with your open kitchen concept, you should. People love fire.

Have a nice wood fired pizza oven? Face the opening towards the dining room, and put a glass wall about ten feet in front of it. Your customers will see inside, to the fire, as well as you being able to prepare and do the dirty work out of sight. Both of these also give you the necessary sound barrier.

There are even pieces of equipment specifically made for display. You can have a massive spinning rack of roast chickens, or just a small kebab spinner. Cool equipment is always fun, just don't go crazy.

Hot Line in Front

This is my least favorite concept. It comes down to a row of people staring intently at some poor sap reducing a sauce or slicing steak. I do understand the appeal. With the advent of food programming and the people cooking on them, there is now more than ever a desire by the masses to watch you cook their filet. There are a few ways to accomplish this.

You could just put enough space for the noise, but that's not ideal. You could also construct a viewing wall. This could be floor to ceiling or just a few feet tall. It could have a bar with a counter. Or tables with windows inset next to them. I always thought it would be cool to have a giant viewing window behind a bar. Neat concept, I've never seen it, but I think you could make it snazzy.

As I said, I understand the concept. You put a bottle of liquor next to everyone on the line and let them light fires all service. The customer will love it. The problem is always in the execution with these types of concepts. They can be made well, with design features like blocking the bottom three feet from view so the customer doesn't ever see inside the low boys. Its little things that take you from a great design to a something that seems patched together.

The biggest issue with most open kitchens, is...

Sound

I have alluded to the importance of implementing a sound design with sound in mind. Heeeey...

Anyway, the noise from the kitchen is intense. Vent hoods pull steam and grease, oven doors slam, heavy steel bottomed pans hit the range, fryers bubble, and the list goes on, it's an acoustic nightmare.

Then there are the cooks. I have had owners get irate when this conversation comes up. I try to explain to them that bad language in a kitchen is as ubiquitous as food in kitchens, but they don't like to listen. Things like 'Everyone needs to watch their mouth' start getting thrown around. I could probably debate for hours on this one, but I'll spare you and keep it short. Owners, please pay attention.

First off, if someone didn't cuss before they started in a kitchen, they will. Let's get that out of the way. Your staff *will* swear and people *will* eventually hear it. I'm sorry to burst your bubble. However in my experience, my preaching this until I'm blue in the face never helps, so how about we make a silent line. I don't care if you bus in a team of people currently undergoing a vow of silence. Eventually, someone is getting fryer oil on their leg and a great F bomb will spread throughout the restaurant. This is embarrassing at the best of times and grounds for litigation in the worst. This is why I always prefer sealed or mostly sealed concepts.

As you have probably noticed, open kitchen simply means people can see in it. You can have a physical barrier in place. This is a great way to go, as you don't have to worry about it.

Your sound level depends on how much space is actually open between the dining room and the kitchen. More open more noise, obvious I know, but needs stating. If you just have a gap in the pass you can get away with a pretty close first table. As the hole gets bigger, people need to be farther away.

Sometimes you want some kitchen noise, and that's ok too. You just need to get going, and see what the sound levels will be in the dining room. This is where experience is valuable. Sure, you could hire some acoustics guy to create a virtual space and run virtual tests, but let's get real. If you have a chef that has worked in a few of these concepts he can tell you from firsthand experience what works and what doesn't. It's never a bad idea to have a failsafe if you need to make it louder or quieter, but you should be fine if you follow the expert you hired.

As with everything, I do suggest going to restaurants already doing something similar to what you want. This can be expensive as not every major city has five of these restaurants, so you might need to travel. You should bring your chef as well. You two need to be on the same page for concepts before all else.

Once you get these basic ideas for sound down, you can even try the white whale, the…

Fully open Concept

No glass, no barriers, nothing between you and every piece of food coming out. But how you may ask. 'Don't we have a group of foul mouthed sailors slinging plates?' Oh yes, and the answer is distance.

I've worked in places like this. One of my favorite designs was as follows.

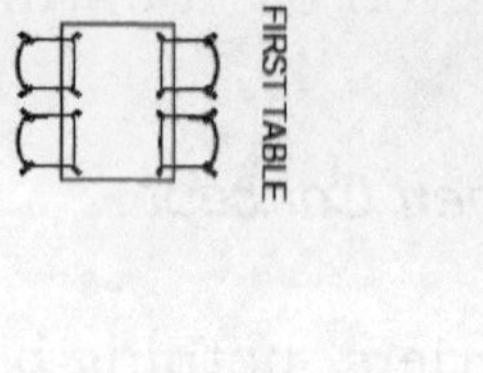
FIRST TABLE

SPECIALITY
ROASTER

GRILL

FLAT TOP

OVEN

MISE EN PLACE / PLATING

MISE EN PLACE / PLATING

FRYERS / GARDE MANGER

PROFESSIONAL KITCHEN DESIGN

As you can see the line is a right angle. The wall in front of the cooks (while facing the customers) is about chest high, holding the mise en place. Behind them is the necessary equipment for that station, with a hood above. The beauty of this design is the simplicity. The chest high wall stops a lot of the noise from utensils hitting equipment and so on, as well as ensuring the back of the person is turned to the customers while preforming louder actions.

You do also have noise reduction while plating, as the plates are dealt with behind the barrier on the pass. Once food is completed, the cook can simply put the plate up on the partition for pick up. In this set up, the chef is actually on the side of the customer during service most of the time. This gives the customer an added feeling of trust, as they can see the man/woman in charge, and watch his/her coordination of the service. His/her voice however, is always projected back into the chasm that is the line.

The point of this design is the distance. The closest table is about twelve meters. Granted you need a very large space to be able to not pack that area with tables, but this is just an example. Not only have you created a chasm for sound to bounce around in and disperse primarily towards the ceiling (made of sound reductive material), but you have enough distance to make most verbal exchanges inaudible.

Although this is not the only way to create an open kitchen design, this was one of the most impressive I have seen to date.

There are always more ways to accomplish a goal, and if a fully open concept is what you truly desire it can be done. You simply need asses the space you have and consider all the variables we have discussed. Lighting, noise levels, budget, what equipment you want to be seen by the customer, how many seats are you willing to give up to accomplish your goal, and will your business benefit from the hassle, need to be carefully considered.

Most of the time, it simply isn't worth the headache. You end up spending too much time trying to accomplish something that at the end of the day, doesn't affect the food. That being said, customer experience is everything, so if you are capable of executing a proper open kitchen, I say go for it. You can elevate your restaurant from a Tuesday lunch location to a date night spot.

Sinks and Sockets

Every station has needs, and sinks and sockets are a perfect start. We already discussed basic set up of a station, but you need to know where your sinks and sockets will be. Every station should have at least two sockets and one sink.

At the bare minimum, every station needs a hand sink. You remember that guy running around the kitchen like a crazy person? His hand sink was on the other side of the kitchen. Some people seem to think that cooks don't care, but that's because good cooks don't make the news. The guy who has been on the line for twenty years and washes his hands after every piece of meat he touches doesn't get recognition, but salmonella Sally does.

You need to look at this logically. If you provide a hand sink for a station and the cook doesn't use it, fire the cook. Cook doesn't have a sink to wash his hands easily, fire the kitchen designer.

PROFESSIONAL KITCHEN DESIGN

Sockets are also essential for any station. The more the better. You don't need to go crazy, but make sure there are at least two per station. This is the twenty first century, so yes we cooks need electricity. They should be convenient but not somewhere that they will collect food. Putting a socket on the wall where a table meets it is the worst placement you can possibly use yet this seems to be the norm. This is one of the biggest tells of a kitchen designer with no experience. Any cook worth his salt will have a story about a kitchen with this set up if you ask.

The problem lies with the inherent cave like nature of the socket. If you are blending a soup or sauce and it splashes, it goes in the hole. If you are chopping something quickly and pieces fly off, they go in the hole. You get the point now I guess. Of course, this is simple right? Just clean it. But cleaning a live electrical socket is never a good idea, and when cleaning a kitchen at night your hands are wet. Either way, don't play with live sockets.

I bet you are wondering where to place your sockets by now eh? Well I have to give the reasoning behind my thoughts or I get an onslaught of 'but whys'. Your placement will depend on what space you have available. My general rule is to keep sockets under the table, but towards an edge. So if you have an appliance with a short cord you can still reach it. I also like protrusions for the sockets themselves. If you have tile, you can come out one tile to make a box. This will stop liquids that hit the wall above the socket a non-issue, depending on how you top the box.

You would be surprised how many people construct kitchens without taking very important aspects into consideration. Yet another reason an experienced chef is needed for proper kitchen design.

General Equipment Shenanigans

The equipment needed for any given restaurant varies so greatly there is no way I can give a one size fits all answer to anyone. What I can do, is give some guidelines that can help bring to light some things that you might not have thought about.

Quality

I will say this once and as clearly as possible. No matter how many owners want to believe otherwise, you need COMMERCIAL KITCHEN EQUIPMENT. So many people want to start a restaurant assuming because things work at home they will work in the professional kitchen. This is not the case, and I refuse to waste more time justifying this fact.

Countertops

Most of the work done in a kitchen is on a counter, so you would think people would care more about them. Your counters are one of the most important assets in the kitchen. How they are designed can change everything from morale to health code rating. Four things make a good countertop, the materials, the junctions, the backsplash, and the ease of cleaning.

Materials are easy, you want stainless steel. There are exceptions of course for specialty purposes such as a marble top for pastry, but for the most part you want stainless steel. I don't mean a wooden table with a stainless steel plate, that's just so many kinds of wrong you deserve to be closed down. I mean all stainless steel. You'll see all shapes and sizes in any catalogue or on restaurant supply website.

The junctions are where the counter meets something. Most kitchens in tight spaces will piece in tables right next to each other, touching to increase space. The problem here is the small gap that is formed.

Things just build up in there. You can help yourself sleep at night by remembering you deep clean once a week and clean it, but it will be gross, always. This also includes junctions with the wall, enter backsplashes.

The backsplash as it refers to countertops is generally a piece of metal that extents from the actual counter. The metal curved up from the back of the counter in a way that forms a smooth curve. This aids in cleaning as you can wipe it easily with a rag. Most backsplashes are around four inches tall. They can get taller, but four to six inches is about all you need. The point isn't to completely block the wall; the point is to stop liquid from going into a crack. If you cut tomatoes for an hour there is a lot of liquid released. Any liquid is potentially dripped into cracks. Follow that up with some meat juices and you see my point.

Ease of cleaning, as with everything else we have discussed is imperative. This goes back to why you don't want a steel plate on a wooden table. You have to keep everything sanitary. You don't want a table with some weird metal pattern under it or a lip of a table that has a lip on it where food can collect. You don't want holes for screws for adjustable shelves, and you don't want something on the feet that will fall apart after a year. Pay attention to any small feature that might be able to collect dust or food particles. Sometimes this could be a table with a weird edge, or a screw head on the side of the leg. You need to pay attention to anything that can get you hit on a health inspection later.

When I am asked my ideal table for a workspace in a restaurant, I like to have the kind of table described above with a bottom shelf and enough space on the side to clean it. Get the right tables and counters, and keep them spaced.

Refrigeration

When I talk about refrigeration, I am mostly talking about walk-ins and reach-ins. Low boys are counters, and some are designed to handle heat. When it comes to your walk ins, you need to place them away from your hot line. Your prepped food for service should be ready and waiting on the line during service. Constant walk in runs should not be necessary. This will also allow you to save costs on cooling.

The best location for a walk in freezer is in the refrigerator. Just in case someone reading hasn't seen this set-up, you walk into your fridge and your freezer door is in there. This helps cut cooling costs. I can't say it's my favorite system to work with, but it makes sense.

Product Processing Hardware

I'm simply referring to your immersion blenders, food processors, stand/bear mixers, immersion circulators, etc. The equipment you use to change the state of a product. I know this is a broad category, and I could go on for days about the differences in the products such as gas vs electric ovens, food processor A vs processor B, or what the quart system is on an immersion blender, but I'm not going to write a five page advertisement.

To put it simply, make sure you buy quality equipment. If you are new to the industry you need to look no further than your chef to find out what equipment is quality. By which I mean your chef should have the experience to know which brands have a track record of excellence and which do not. Most common kitchen equipment is available in all countries. If you happen to be in a country that doesn't have what you are looking for, I suggest importing what you need. You can buy off brand equipment that is available to you in your area, but I don't suggest it.

Heat

As obvious as it is, it needs stating that you will have to have vent hoods over all equipment producing heat and/or steam. Shocking, I know. This means you will have to keep your hot line contained to a certain area or areas.

This is not only because of vent hoods, but it is also much easier to run connections for equipment to one area and branch it from there.

I am not able to get into details on what you need, but I can tell you for most pot and pan cooking I prefer a French top. I believe I have professed my love for the contraption in at least one of my other works.

Your stations and menu will ultimately decide what equipment you will need and where it will need to be placed, but there is more to it than that. You have to consider multiple aspects of each piece of equipment.

Hinges

You need to think about the little details. Such as which way the oven door will open. It may seem like a small detail, but if your oven door constantly blocks a station or a walkway, you could run into issues during services.

How will your fryer door open? Will it be easy to access for cleaning or will it be blocked by a wall. You need to know what equipment you will be purchasing and know about all the little details before designing something that isn't practical.

Safety

This is a pretty broad subject obviously, but you do need to think about safety when designing a kitchen. You cannot just put a fryer next to an open flame for example. Depending on where you are in the world, there might be standards in the industry, but you will have to look into that wherever you are. A quick call to the fire marshal might inform you that fryers need to be at least one meter from an open flame, for example. Finding out what the fire codes are in your area is important, and need to be taken into account.

Behind

You also need to consider what is behind your hot line. You need to make sure whatever is there can stand up to the heat of the equipment. I know this seems obvious, but these are the kinds of things you need to know going into your project.

Air conditioning

Air conditioning in a kitchen is nice, but expensive. In America it is commonplace, however many places don't even consider it as an option. Whether or not you use it is up to you, however if you don't have it, a window is something to consider. A nice cold breeze from outside can be nice in a stuffy kitchen. At least then you can tell your staff you did something to reduce the heat.

End

There are so many intricacies when designing a proper kitchen there is no way for me to cover everything. All you really need to know is your concept. You and your chef need to know the kind of food and service you will be presenting the customer as well as what it takes to accomplish it. The concept can be discussed early on, so ask questions and be open. You need ask your potential chef what he/she thinks about what we have discussed. Ask him/her what he/she thinks about socket placement, or restaurant acoustics, and judge their responses. Do they know what they are talking about, or are they faking it? Once you get a good chef, trust him/her. There is a lot of work to do, and you have hired someone to make decisions, let them make those decisions. They can explain the whys, you just have to listen.

PROFESSIONAL KITCHEN DESIGN

Tristan B. Jones

To whom it may concern,

I hope these three books, as well as BBB, have helped you on your path to a happy and prosperous career in restaurants. Most people will never understand how much work goes into a new restaurant, and never will. Corporations have the upper hand by having systems in place that you simply cannot obtain without corporate might.

More and more franchised restaurants are taking over our local landscapes. Some chant capitalism and others scream subsidies, but the fact remains. Many of these companies are succeeding because a local restaurant failed solely based on ignorance and pride.

By reading my books, I know you are trying to do everything right. You are doing research in an attempt to better the lives of your employees as well as yourself. I salute you, I truly do, and from the bottom of my heart, hope you succeed.

Tristan B Jones

Tristan B. Jones

For further information I am available
for consultation at

Chef.tristan.jones@gmail.com

PROFESSIONAL KITCHEN DESIGN

Tristan B. Jones

DRAW YOUR DESIGN

PROFESSIONAL KITCHEN DESIGN

DRAW YOUR DESIGN

Tristan B. Jones

DRAW YOUR DESIGN

PROFESSIONAL KITCHEN DESIGN

DRAW YOUR DESIGN

89

Tristan B. Jones

DRAW YOUR DESIGN

PROFESSIONAL KITCHEN DESIGN

DRAW YOUR DESIGN

91

Tristan B. Jones